BIBLE
Baby
Names

BIBLE
Baby
Names

Spiritual Choices from

Judeo-Christian Tradition

Anita Diamant

For People of All Faiths, All Backgrounds

JEWISH LIGHTS PUBLISHING • WOODSTOCK, VERMONT

Bible Baby Names: Spiritual Choices from Judeo-Christian Tradition
© 1996 by Anita Diamant

Library of Congress Cataloging-in-Publication Data
Diamant, Anita.
   Bible baby names : spiritual choices from Judeo-Christian tradition / Anita Diamant.
         p.   cm.
   Includes bibliographical references.
   ISBN 1-879045-62-1 (pb)
   1. Names, Personal—Dictionaries. 2. Names in the Bible—
Dictionaries.   I. Title.
CS2377.D49 1996
929.4'4—dc20   96-25012
                                                      CIP

10 9 8 7 6 5 4 3 2 1

Manufactured in the United States of America
Cover design & illustration by Annette Compton
Text design by Karen Savary

For People of All Faiths, All Backgrounds
J e w i s h   L i g h t s   P u b l i s h i n g
A Division of LongHill Partners, Inc.
P.O. Box 237 / Sunset Farm Offices, Rte. 4
Woodstock, Vermont 05091
Tel: (802) 457-4000 Fax: (802) 457-4004

For Margaret

Contents

Acknowledgments   *9*

Introduction   *11*

A Son! Bible Names for Boys   27

A Daughter! Bible Names for Girls   77

Resources   *121*

Notes   *123*

Acknowledgments

Thanks to Stuart Matlins at Jewish Lights for the idea for *Bible Baby Names* and for his friendship. Thank you also to Sandra Korinchak at Jewish Lights for her unfailingly cheerful assistance and support on this book.

Thanks to all librarians, everywhere, always.

Introduction

"Be fruitful and multiply" is the first biblical commandment to humankind. Perhaps then, it should come as no surprise that nothing in life puts you in touch with God like having a baby. Anyone who's ever been in a delivery room knows that birth is a miracle—a literal, honest-to-goodness holy miracle. Adoptive parents, holding their child for the first time, feel the same overwhelming wonder as they count fingers and toes and blessings.

Giving a name to the miracle that is your baby is no trivial matter. Choosing your baby's name is, in a way, a second conception—an act of creation that hearkens back to the beginning of creation. Early in the book of Genesis, God brings the newly formed animals to Adam "to see what he would call them" (Genesis 2:19). Naming is thus portrayed as the first independent human act.

Adam's job in Eden was to name the beasts of the field, the birds of the air, and every living thing. This was no make-work project. The Hebrew for "word," *davar*, is also the Hebrew for "thing," suggesting the close connection between a name and the character or essence of the named.

Giving a child a name intuitively confirms this religious insight, which is common to virtually all human communities.[1] Naming a baby feels like a self-fulfilling prophecy; a beautiful name will predict a beautiful soul, a strong name suggests endurance. Like Adam's task in the Garden of Eden, giving the "right" name to your baby is an exercise of creative power, mandated by God yet also expressive of your tastes, your history, and your dreams for your child.

According to an ancient Jewish saying, "With each child, the world begins anew." The name you select will help to shape the person your child will become and the world he or she will create. By deciding to make this important choice within a biblical context, you are giving your child an identity, a community, and a way of living in the world that is informed by religious priorities and insights. This is a great gift.

God was pleased with Adam's choice of names. May God be pleased with your choices, too.

What's in a Bible Name?

While a rose by any other name might well smell as sweet, people are more complicated than roses. People are a mix of nature and nurture, of education and environment. People who are loved tend to be loving; children who hear English spoken at home learn to speak English. A child named Tiffany inherits a legacy of worldly beauty and material elegance. A baby named Martha, on the other hand, receives an altogether different kind of inheritance—one which will eventually lead to her to the Bible to look up her namesake, and perhaps to other books and stories about the biblical Martha.

Every name is a complicated gift, but biblical names tend to be among the richest. For one thing, they are often family names, handed down from one generation to the next. If you name your baby Peter or Rebecca in honor of Grandpa Pete or Great-Aunt Becky, your child becomes a living link to their namesakes, and to Pete and Becky's namesakes before them, all the way back to the biblical Peter and Rebecca.

How and why you chose a particular name will eventually be of enormous interest to your child. Children love to hear stories about themselves, and the origin of a name makes a fascinating tale. Someday, you will tell your Ruth or Simon about the names you considered and rejected, about the day you found their name in this very book, about Great-Grandmother Ruth and Uncle Simon, and about their biblical namesakes. The more numerous and meaningful your stories, the better, since you will be asked to tell them again and again and again as your children grow.

The Bible—especially the Hebrew Bible*—stresses the importance of names and naming in several stories. Abram and Sarai become Abraham and Sarah after they accept the covenant with God; only after that do they become the ancestors of a multitude, the founders of the Hebrew nation, the progenitors of Judaism and Christianity. Even more striking is the name change of Jacob, which means "supplanter" and refers to Jacob's victorious struggle with his twin brother, Esau. But after Jacob contends with an angel, he gets a completely new name—Israel (wrestler with God), and becomes the patriarch of the 12 tribes of Israel.

Proverb 22 says, "A good name is rather to be chosen than good oil," oil being a measure of wealth.

*The terms "Hebrew Bible" and "Christian Bible" are used throughout this book in lieu of "Old Testament" and "New Testament," out of respect for the fact that Jews acknowledge no "new" testament that supersedes an "old" one.

"A good name" refers to reputation, but throughout the Bible there is a sense that names have an inherent value and power. In the Christian Bible, the most dramatic name change is not all that obvious; when Jesus refers to God as Father, he uses the familiar, tender form "Abba" or Daddy and thus makes God seem more accessible.

In the Gospels, Jesus' name itself becomes an emblem and proof of faith, with the power to sanctify those who invoke it; "And Jesus...took a child and set him by him. And said unto them, Whosoever shall receive this child in my name receiveth me" (Luke 9:47–48).

Throughout their histories, Jews and Christians have always turned to the Bible for baby names—though by no means exclusively, as witnessed by all the Melissas and Bradleys on the Sunday school rolls. Nevertheless, scripture has been a constant source of inspiration and identity. It is said that, during the Egyptian captivity, the Hebrew slaves maintained their sense of identity by holding fast to their own names. When Christians have been in the minority—in Islamic countries, for example—clearly "Christian" names (Mark, Paul, Mary) were favored as a way of preserving their distinctive identity, too. During the Reformation, Protestants used names from the Hebrew Bible as a way of distinguishing themselves from Catholics, who baptized their infants with the names of saints, as decreed by the Council of Trent.[2]

Names in the Bible

There are more than 2,800 personal names in the Hebrew Bible; approximately 500 in the Christian Bible. Few of these—perhaps no more than five percent—are in use today.[3]

While about half of the people mentioned in the Bible have a unique name—there is only one Abraham—some names are borne by several or even many others; for example, there are eight Philips, ten Michaels, 25 Johns and 30 Zechariahs.[4] And some biblical characters seem to have more than one name: Peter is also referred to as Cephas and Simon.

The vast majority of names in the Bible are Hebrew in origin, but there are a smattering from other languages, including Akkadian, Aramean, Egyptian, Greek, and Latin. Biblical names that "sound" Muslim—Jazreel, for example—reflect the fact that most of the languages of the biblical past share common roots with modern Arabic.

Regardless of their origin, all biblical names do have a meaning, a "definition" of sorts. Sometimes, these are connected with character, temperament, or the person's historical role; Naomi means "my sweetness," Andrew means "virile." Eve's name comes from the root word for life, *hai*. (Hava is the Hebrew version of Eve.)

Several biblical names are explained within scripture, though these tend to be offered more as description or story explanation than as literal definition. Moses is translated in the Bible as meaning "because I drew him out of the water" (Exodus 2:10). When Leah, Jacob's unloved wife, bears her first child, she calls him Reuben and explains that her baby's name means, "Surely the Lord hath looked upon my affliction now therefore my husband will love me" (Genesis 30:32).

Not all names are endowed with historical significance or character references. Animal names are not uncommon; Caleb means "dog"; Rebecca means "ewe." The Bible is, in fact, full of names taken from nature, which to North American ears, resonate with Native American associations: Deborah means "bee"; Jonah means "dove"; Barak means "lightning"; Rhoda means "rose." This tradition has been revived with a passion in modern Israel where popular names include Tal and Tali ("dew"), Elon and Elana ("oak"), Oren ("fir tree"), and Namir ("leopard"). Sometimes, the name of a city or town is used as a personal name, as is the case with Lydia and Boaz.

While the natural world is a source of biblical inspiration, many more Bible names are theophoric, which is to say that they exalt God. Names with the prefix or suffix *el, eli, ya, yahu* all refer to the Holy One: Elisha—"My God is salvation"; Raphael—"God has healed."

The people named in the Bible represent the whole gamut of humanity: the good, the bad, the saintly, the corrupt, heroes and prophets, executioners and martyrs, kings, priests, soldiers, prophets, builders and musicians, the great and the obscure. Sometimes all we know of a biblical character is his, and far less often, her, name.

Men's names far outnumber women's names in the Bible: about 3,000 to fewer than 200. The Christian Bible lists 150 disciples of Jesus—30 of whom are women—a statistical shift that some scholars believe reflects the importance of women in the early days of the church.

The Bible's patriarchal bias is most evident in the long lists of "begats" that record fathers and sons but rarely mention mothers, wives, or sisters. There are few female prophets, warriors, prophetesses and priests, and their names tend to be well-known: Miriam, Deborah, Esther, Judith. Nearly all biblical women are identified in relationship to a husband or son, as is the case with the matriarchs of the Hebrew Bible. However, many women in the Bible are referred to without any name, such as the daughters of Jethro and the wife of Noah.

While a number of women in the Christian Bible have independent relationships with Jesus (Mary Magdalene, Mary of Bethany), and others are identified as part of early Christian families (Priscilla and her husband Aquila), their numbers are few and some—such as the four daughters of Philip the evangelist—are mentioned but nameless.

Choosing Your Baby's Name

Baby names are as susceptible to fashion as hemlines. In every generation, some names become popular and others drop out of use altogether. And although some biblical names are perennials (Michael, for example, has a seemingly permanent spot on the list of "ten favorite boys' names"), Bible names that were considered unthinkably quaint and dated a generation ago have been reclaimed with a vengeance, as a quick count of the Sarahs, Hannahs, Nathaniels, and Zacharys in the neighborhood nursery school will attest.

The Bible offers a roster that ranges from the familiar to the exotic. Some Bible names are instantly recognizable: John, Paul and Joanna, for instance; some are slightly more unusual, but still well within the realm of comfort, such as Jordan, Nathan, and Abigail. Other biblical names require a bit more courage, a desire to distinguish your child, and a willingness to correct misspellings: Jahleel, Zilla, and Cyrene.

African-Americans have, since the days of slavery, plumbed the scriptures—especially the Hebrew Bible—for names and helped to reclaim and return to popular use many beautiful and indeed powerful ones, including Moses and Isaiah, Arna and Zora.

African-American naming patterns, while still cutting-edge, now fit into a larger shift toward a full celebration of ethnic diversity. This change means that interesting and even unusual names are not necessarily a burden for children. A child with a biblical name such as Tovia or Nerius will probably feel right at home in class with kids who answer to An, Takako, and Ahmed.

In Israel, where Hebrew is a living language, there has been a surge in the use of ancient biblical names that had not been heard for generations, such as Amnon, Yoram, Avital, Tamar, and even Aviram, who was swallowed by the earth in retribution for his instigation of the rebellion against Moses. The content of biblical stories doesn't necessarily keep parents from using a particular name; thus ill-fated Dina and little-known Naphtali are beautiful, fashionable, and popular.

Generally, parents don't select a name based on its etymology or definition or even its biblical association. Nobody thinks you're calling your daughter a sheep if you call her Rachel, even though the name is derived from the Hebrew word for "ewe." Names are not predictors of behavior. Leah, which means "weariness," does not condemn a child to perpetual lethargy. Nor is any name a guarantee of any sort. Although many fine men have been called Joseph, fiends have also borne the name. In other words, your child is the one who will determine whether his or her name is a "good name" in the sense meant in Ecclesiastes (7:1): "A good name is better than precious ointment." Of course, there are some names that are simply too laden with negative images—too poisoned by association— to hang on a poor baby. Ahab? No way.

About the List

This book does not contain a complete or comprehensive list of every personal name that appears in the Bible. This is not a scholarly work or a definitive dictionary.[5] The names you will find here reflect the author's best effort to catalog biblical names that conform to current American tastes and trends—but which also "push the envelope" a bit. While this list is unabashedly idiosyncratic, criteria were applied to the selection process.

For example:

Writing the name "Jezebel" on a birth certificate is like pinning a permanent "Kick me" sign on a child's back. Thus, the wanton Jezebel, the traitorous Judas, and the evil Amalek are not included, nor are the villains Herod and Haman, nor is Salome, who demanded the head of John the Baptist on a plate.

Azazel—a demon—is not listed. On the other hand, Lilith, also a demon, is included not only because it is such a pretty name, but because ancient stories about Lilith as Adam's first wife (before Eve) are so intriguing.

The sound, spelling, and complexity of names was a primary determinant in deciding what to include and what to leave out. Shephupham[6] is not here because it's such an awful mouthful. (The fact that it means "viper" didn't help either.) On the other hand, Saphira is included because it is a lovely name—even if the character herself came to an evil end because of love of money.

Nothing is known about many biblical characters whose names appear once in a list of "begats" and are never mentioned again; Hadlai, for example, is noted as the father of Amasa, who was one four officers who showed mercy to a group of Judean captives (Second Chronicles 28:12). Apart from raising a decent son, we know nothing more of Hadlai, yet his name fits into an English-speaking context much better than that of his admirable son. And so Hadlai is included, while Amasa is not.

Since there are so many fewer names for girls than for boys, filling out a list of options for daughters included using names and nouns that appear in some form in the Bible though not necessarily as personal names: Ora ("light"), Leila ("night"), Gila ("joy"), Rimona ("pomegranate"). Place names are also used for girls: Giah, Myra, Sharona, Shiloh. Many of these names are in current use as girls' names in Israel today.

Hebrew, like English, often employs the same name for boys and for girls: Yona ("dove"), Ayal and Ayala ("deer"), Liron and Lirona ("song"). As in English, it is common practice to feminize boys' names by adding a final vowel: Gabriel becomes Gabriella. Jonathan becomes Jonatha. And in some cases, men's names that simply sound feminine in English—for example, Beri and Yafia—are offered as selections for girls.

Key to the List

Language and Definitions

- All translations are from Hebrew unless otherwise noted.
- All names are given in their English/Anglicized form first; in some cases, a Hebrew version will follow: Gilead, Gilad (Gee-lahd)
- A literal translation is given, followed by a brief description of a biblical character who bore the name, and a citation.
- Biblical citations correspond to the King James version of the Bible.

- The citation noted may be the only place the name appears in the Bible, or only one of many. Check a concordance for further references.

- No citation appears in cases where:

  —the entry refers to another name, which is cited: for example, Joelle, Joella, the feminine version of Joel.

  —the name is derived from a noun rather than a name; this occurs with some frequency in the list for daughters, i.e., Kitra ("crown").

Spelling

- All English versions of Bible names are transliterations from other languages that use different alphabets. This means that spelling is, to some extent, flexible.

- The most common spelling is given first, followed by alternatives where they are used or may help with general pronunciation, for example: Dina, Dinah, Dena, Deena.

- Choose the spelling you prefer, or make up your own.

- The final "h" on names ending with a vowel (Sarah) can be dropped (Sara).

Pronunciation

- A pronunciation guide is provided for unusual or unfamiliar names.

• Assume that the emphasis falls on the last syllable for Hebrew names. Adam, for instance, is
Ah-*dahm*. Sarah is Sah-*rah*. In English, however,
the emphasis usually moves to the first syllable.
As in Adam and Sarah.

• When a pronunciation guide appears, the first
example is true to the Hebrew and the second
choice, when given, is how the name is likely to
be spoken in English; for example, Irijah (Ee-
ree-*yah*, Ear-*eye*-jah).

• It is possible to transform some well-known
English names back to a more authentic biblical
pronunciation through spelling and usage.
Davide, for instance, will be Dah-*veed*, if the
final "e" is added and that is what his parents
call him from infancy.

• There is no soft "ch" sound (as in Charles) in
the Hebrew language. The guttural "ch," which
is typically Hebrew, has been Anglicized (made
into English) by substituting the letter "h" (as in
Hannah, for example).

• English tends to render the Hebrew sound "v"
into "b" (Avigail becomes Abigail).

• English tends to render initial Hebrew's initial
"Y" into "J" (Yonah becomes Jonah).

A Son!
Bible Names
for Boys

Aaron *(Ah-ha-roan)*

Teaching, singing, shining, or mountain. (Messenger in Aramaic.) The brother of Moses and Miriam, the first Israelite high priest. (Exodus 4:14)

Abdon

Little servant. One of the "lesser" judges. (Judges 12:13)

Abednigo *(Ah-bed-nih-go)*
Servant of the God Nego. (Aramaic) A name given to Daniel's companion, Hananiah, by King Nebuchanezzar. (Daniel 1:7) Abednigo, with Meshach and Shadrach, survived terrible trials for his faith.

Abel
Breath. The son of Adam and Eve. (Genesis 4:2)

Abidan
Father-judge. A son of Gidioni. (Numbers 2:22)

Abiel *(Ah-bee-el)*
God is my father. Grandfather of King Saul. (First Samuel 9:1)

Abiezer *(Ah-bee-eh-zer)*
My father is help. Son of Manasseh. (Joshua 17:2)

Abihu *(Ah-bee-hu)*
My Father is He. One of Aaron's sons. (Exodus 6:23)

Abijah *(Ah-bee-yah, or Ah-buy-jah)*
My father God. Younger son of Samuel, also a judge. (First Samuel 8:2)

Abner, Avner*
Literally, father of light. Avner ben Ner was King Saul's cousin and the commander of his army. (First Samuel 17:55)

> * In Hebrew "av" (generally Anglicized as "ab") means "father."

Abraham, Avraham

Father of a mighty nation, or as God defines the name, "Father of many nations have I made thee." The first Hebrew. (Genesis 17:5)

Abram, Avram

Exalted father. Abraham's original name, which was changed with the addition of the Hebrew letter H (hay) which appears twice in the unpronounceable name of God (YHVH). (Genesis 11:26)

Absalom

Father of peace. King David's son, famous for his great beauty. (Second Samuel 14:25)

Adam

Of red earth. (Mankind in Phoenician and Babylonian.) The first man. (Genesis 2:7)

Adin *(Ah-deen, Ay-din)*

Beautiful, pleasant, gentle. An Israelite leader whose sons return from the exile in Babylonia. (Ezra 2:15)

Adlai

Refuge of God. (Aramaic) A shepherd for King David. (First Chronicles 27:29)

Alexander

He who protects men. (Greek) Alexander the Great is mentioned in First Maccabees (1:1). Other men bearing this name appear in Mark (15:21), Acts (4:6) and elsewhere in the Christian Bible.

Allon, Alon *(Ah-lone, Ah-lahn)*
Oak tree. One of the sons of Simeon. Also spelled Elon, Elam. (First Chronicles 4:37)

Alvan
Height. First of the five sons of Shobal. (Genesis 36:23)

Alyan *(Ahl-yahn)*
Heights. One of the sons of Seir. (First Chronicles 1:40)

Amal *(Ah-mahl)*
Work. A member of the tribe of Asher. (First Chronicles 7:35)

Amiel *(Ah-mee-el)*
God of my people. The father of Machir, who was a friend of King David. (Second Samuel 9:4)

Amir *(Ah-meer)*
Mighty, strong.

Amitai *(Ah-mee-tie)*
True, faithful. The father of Jonah. (Jonah 1:1)

Amnon
Faithful. A son of King David. (Second Samuel 3:2)

Amos

Strong. One of the prophets who preached social morality, Amos began his life as a shepherd. (Amos) Another Amos is mentioned as an ancestor of Jesus. (Luke 3:25)

Amram

A mighty nation. The father of Moses, Miriam and Aaron. (Exodus 6:18)

Andrew

The virile one. (Greek) One of the four privileged disciples (with Peter, James, and John) he was among the fishermen called by Jesus to the lake to become a "fisher of men." (Matthew 4:18)

Andronicus

Conqueror of men. (Greek) A Roman Christian, a relative of Paul and his companion in captivity. (Romans 16:7)

Apollos

Beautiful man. (Greek sun god) An early Christian teacher from Alexandria. (Acts 18:24)

Aquila *(Ah-key-la)*

Eagle. (Latin) An early follower of Jesus who, with his wife Prisca or Priscilla, met Paul at Corinth. (Acts 18:2)

Aram
From the Assyrian for "heights." The ancient name of Syria. Also, a grandson of Noah. (Genesis 10:23)

Aran *(Ah-rahn)*
Chest, as in box. (Arabic) A son of Seir. (Genesis 36:28)

Ariel
Lion of God. A leader who served under Ezra; also a poetic name for the city of Jerusalem. (Ezra 8:16)

Asa
Healer. The third king of Judah, who reigned for 41 years. (First Kings 15:8)

Asaiah *(Ah-see-yah, or Ay-zay-yah)*
God has made. A common biblical name. (First Chronicles 6:14)

Asher
Blessed, fortunate. The son of Jacob and Zilpah, Leah's handmaiden, and the leader of one of the 12 tribes of Israel. (Genesis 30:13)

Augustus, August
Revered, exalted. (Latin) The Roman emperor Caesar Augustus is mentioned in Luke 2:1.

Azarel
God has helped. An ally of David, before he became king. (First Chronicles 12:6)

Azariah *(Ah-zar-ee-ah)*
God has helped. There are many Azariahs; the first was a grandson of Jacob's son, Judah, and his wife, Zerah (First Chronicles 2:8). Another biblical Azariah was renamed Abednego in Daniel.

Azriel *(Az-ree-el)*
God is my help. A member of the family of Manasseh. (First Chronicles 5:24)

Balak *(Bah-lahk)*
To destroy. The son of Tzipor, king of Moab. (Numbers 22:2)

Bani *(Bah-nee)*
Son or build. Bani the Gadite was one of David's supporters. (Second Samuel 23:36)

Barak *(Bah-rak)*
Lightning. A biblical soldier and one of the liberators of Israel. (Judges 5:1)

Barnabus, Barnaby
A plea or sermon. (Latin, Greek) "Son of consolation" is the biblical explanation. A disciple of Paul. (Acts 4:36)

Bartholomew
"Son of Talmai." (Aramic and Hebrew) One of the 12 disciples. (Matthew 10:3)

Baruch, Baruk *(Bah-rook)*
Blessed. A friend and secretary to the prophet Jeremiah. (Jeremiah 32:12)

Bela *(Bay-lah)*
Swallowed up. The first son of Benjamin. (Genesis 46:21)

Ben
Son of. Ben- is a prefix that is added to many biblical names, hence Ben-Michael, Ben-Ezra, etc.

Benaiah *(Ben-ee-yah, Ben-eye-yah)*
God builds. A common biblical name. One of David's warriors and a commander of his bodyguard. (Second Samuel 23:20)

Benjamin
Son of my right hand. The younger of Rachel's sons and Jacob's favorite. Before she died giving birth, Rachel called him "Ben-oni," son of my sorrow; Jacob changed it to Benjamin. (Genesis 35:18)

Beno
His son. A Levite of the Merari family. (First Chronicles 24:26)

Beri
My well. The father of the prophet Hosea. (Hosea 1:1)

Bezalel *(Beh-zah-lel)*
In the shadow of God. A descendent of Judah considered the ancestor of all artists, he was charged with constructing the ark of the covenant and all of its elaborate and beautiful furnishings. (Exodus 31:2)

Boaz
Strength and swiftness. The great-grandfather of King David and an ancestor of Jesus, Boaz was a wealthy, land-owning Bethlehemite who married Ruth. (Ruth 2:1)

Caleb
Heart, also dog. Of the 12 spies sent by Moses to Canaan, only Caleb and Joshua brought back a favorable report. He became the leader of Israel after the death of Moses. (Numbers 13:6)

Carmi *(Cahr-mee)*
My vine. A son of Reuben and grandson of Jacob. (Genesis 46:9)

Cheran* *(He-ron, Che-ron)*
A son of Dishon, grandson of Seir. (First Chronicles 1:41)

Claudius
Lame. (Latin) Claudius Lysias rescued Paul from persecution. (Acts 21:31)

Clement
Merciful. (Latin) A Christian of Philippi. (Philippians 4:3)

Cornelius
Long life. (Latin) A centurion stationed in Caesarea who became a Christian. (Acts 10:1) Cornel and Cornell are variations.

Crispus
Curly-haired. (Latin) An early Christian who lived in Corinth and was baptized by Paul. (Acts 18:8)

Cyrus
Sun. (Persian) A king of Persia who defeated the Babylonians and permitted the Hebrews to return from exile to Palestine. (Ezra 1:1)

* Many Hebrew names begin with a guttural Hebrew "ch" sound that is not used in English. These tend to be Anglicized as "h" names.

Dan
Judge. Dan was the fifth son of Jacob, and first-born of Bilhah, Rachel's maidservant. (Genesis 30:6)

Daniel
God is my judge. The hero of the Book of Daniel was an interpreter of visions who predicted the future triumph of a Messianic kingdom. (Daniel)

Darius
One who upholds the good. (Greek) A king of Persia who authorized the Jews to carry on the reconstruction of the Temple. (Ezra 5:5)

Darkon *(Dark-ahn)*
To walk quickly. One of the returnees from the Babylonian exodus. (Ezra 2:56)

Datan *(Daht-ahn)*
Degree or law. A member of the tribe of Reuben who conspired against Moses and Aaron. (Numbers 16:25)

David, Davide *(Dah-veed)*
Beloved. David, the shepherd who killed Goliath, was king of Israel and the reputed author of many psalms. He is viewed as an archetype as well as an ancestor of Jesus. (First Samuel 17:12)

Dekar, Deker *(Deh-care)*
To pierce. Ben-Deker (the son of Deker) was an officer of King Solomon. (First Kings 4:9)

Demetrius
Of Demeter (Greek goddess of agriculture). An early Christian missionary. (Third John 12)

Devir *(Deh-veer)*
Holy place. Devir was a king of Eglon in the time of Joshua. (Joshua 10:3)

Dishan, Dishon
Threshed, threshing. Son of Seir. (Genesis 36:21)

Dotan *(Doe-tahn)*
Law. A town in ancient Palestine. (Genesis 37:17)

Ebenezer, Evenezer *(Eh-ben-eh-zer)*
Stone of help. A place name, the site of confrontations between the Israelites and Philistines. (First Samuel 4:1) Eben and Evan are derivatives.

Elam *(Eh-lahm, Ee-lem)*
Eternal. A grandson of Noah. (Genesis 10:22)

Elazar, Eleazar*
God has helped. Aaron's third son and high priest after him. (Exodus 6:23) In Greek, the name is Lazarus.

Eli, Ely
Ascend. Eli was a high priest and the last of the Judges in the days of Samuel. (First Samuel 1:19)

Eliakim *(El-ee-ah-keem)*
My God sets upright. Several biblical men bear this name, including a military man, a king, a trumpeter-priest and two ancestors of Jesus. (Luke 3:30)

Eliezer *(El-ee-eh-zer)*
My God is help. A common biblical name and variant of Elazar. Abraham's steward (Genesis 15:2) and Moses' son (Exodus 18:4).

Elihu *(El-ee-hoo)*
He is my God. A prominent figure in the Book of Job. (32:2)

Elijah
The Lord is my God. Elijah the prophet led the fight against the cult of Baal and ascended to heaven in a chariot of fire but did not die. (Second Kings 1:10) Elie

*El means God. Eli, "my God," is a prefix that is added to dozens of biblical names; for example, Eliav (My God is father), Eliad (God is eternal), Eliam (God is my people), Eliphaz (My God is golden), Elizur (My God is a rock).

in French, Elia in Italian. English versions include Eliot, Ellis, and Elias. Elya is an Israeli nickname.

Elisha

My God is salvation. Successor to the prophet Elijah; many miracles are attributed to Elisha. (First Kings 19:16)

Elkanah *(El-kah-nah)*

God has created. The best-known of many Elkanahs in the Bible was the husband of Peninah and the barren Hannah. (First Samuel 1:1)

Elon

Oak. See Alon.

Emmanuel

God is with us. A symbolic name signifying a descendent of David, and thus, the messiah. (Matthew 1:23) Also spelled Immanuel.

Enoch

Dedicated. Enoch (the Anglicized version of Hanoch) was Cain's son, born after Abel died. (Genesis 4:17)

Enos

Man. Son of Seth, father of Kenan. (Genesis 4:26) Also mentioned as an ancestor of Jesus. (Luke 3:38)

Ephraim, Ephrem
Fruitful. One of Joseph's two sons with Asenath. (Genesis 41:52)

Ephron
Bird. A Hittite from whom Abraham buys a burial site. (Genesis 23:8) Also a place name.

Eran
Industrious. A great-grandson of Joseph. (Numbers 26:36)

Ethan
Strong. A grandson of Judah. (First Chronicles 2:6) An Anglicized verson of Etan or Eitan *(Ay-tahn)*.

Ezekiel
God will strengthen. Ezekiel was a prophet who saw amazing visions of God and described them in vividly personal language. (Ezekiel) Zeke is a pet name.

Ezra
Help. A priest and scribe who led the return from Babylon to Jerusalem, where he became a key figure in the reconstruction of the Temple. (Ezra)

Ezri
My help. One of King David's men. (First Chronicles 27:26)

Felix
Happy. (Latin) Husband of Drusilla, who heard Paul speak. (Acts 24:24)

Festus
Festive, merry. (Latin) Procurator of Judea who had dealings with Paul. (Acts 24:27)

Gabriel, Gavriel
God is my strength. Gabriel was an angel who visited Daniel. (Daniel 8:16)

Gad
Fortunate. Gad was one of Jacob's sons, born to Leah's handmaiden, Zilpah. (Genesis 30:11)

Gaddiel *(Gad-ee-el)*
My Fortune is God. A clan leader of the tribe of Zebulun. (Numbers 13:10)

* These names all begin with a hard "g," as in "good." The soft "g," as in "George," is an Anglicization.

Gamaliel *(Gam-ah-lee-el)*
God is my reward. A leader of the tribe of Manasseh. (Numbers 2:20) Gamaliel the Elder was a Pharisee who helped get the Apostles released. (Acts 5:34)

Garon
Threshing floor.

Gedalia, Gedalya
God is great. A common biblical name; one was a governor of Judea. (Second Kings 25:22)

Gershom
I was a stranger there. Moses named his older son Gershom, referring to the Egyptian captivity. (Exodus 2:22)

Gershon, Gerson
Variations on Gershom. First son of Levi. (Genesis 46:11)

Gibar, Gibbar *(Gee-bahr)*
Strong. One of the returnees from Babylonia. (Ezra 2:20)

Gidel, Gidell
To raise up. A returnee from the Babylonian exile. (Ezra 2:47) Gidal is a variant spelling.

Gideon
A mighty warrior. A fighter and a judge. (Judges 6:11)
The Hebrew is Gidon.

Gil, Gill
Joy.

Gilead, Gilad *(Gee-lahd)*
A place name: a mountain range east of the Jordan
River. (Genesis 31:21) The Hebrew form is Gilad.

Gomer *(Go-mare)*
Fulfillment. One of the seven sons of Japhet. (Genesis
10:2) Also a feminine name in the Bible. (Hosea 1:3)

Hadar *(Hah-dahr)*
Beautiful or adorned. A biblical king of Edom, also
known as Hadad. (Genesis 36:39)

Hadlai
Father of Asama, an officer. (Second Chronicles 28:12)

Haggai
Festival. One of the prophets. (Haggai)

Hananiah *(Hah-nahn-ee-ah)*
The compassion of God. There are many biblical

Hananiahs (also given as Ananiah). One was a prophet during the time of King Zedekiah. (Jeremiah 28:1) Hanan *(Hah-nahn)* is an abbreviated form of this name.

Haran *(Hah-rahn)*
Brother of Abraham. (Genesis 11:26) Also a place name.

Haref, Harif *(Hah-ref, Hah-reef)*
Sharp. A descendant of Caleb. (First Chronicles 2:51)

Harel *(Hahr-el)*
Mountain of God. A biblical place name.

Harim *(Hah-reem)*
Consecrated, sacred. A priest in the time of Nehemiah. (Nehemiah 10:6)

Hermes
Sun. (Greek) A Christian of Rome. (Romans 16:14)

Hermon *(Hair-moan)*
Sacred place. A place name that appears several times in the Bible. (Psalms 89:12, 133:3)

Hezekiah
My strength is God. There are several biblical Hezekiahs, including a king of Judah (Second Kings 18:1), who is listed as an ancestor of Jesus (Matthew 1:9). Zeke is a nickname.

Hiram

Noble-born. King of Tyre, a contemporary of Solomon and David, who helped plan, build, and equip the Temple in Jerusalem. (Second Chronicles 2:3)

Hosea *(Hoe-she-yah)*

God hears. One of the minor prophets. (Hosea)

Ichabod

Where is glory. Son of Phineas, grandson of Eli. (First Samuel 4:21)

Ilai *(Ee-lie)*

Superior. One of David's warriors. (First Chronicles 11:29)

Ilan *(Ee-lahn)*

Tree. An alternative transliteration for Alon.

Immanuel

See Emmanuel.

Imri *(Im-ree)*

My word. A member of the tribe of Judah. (First Chronicles 9:4)

Ira
Swiftness. (Arabic) One of King David's soldiers. (Second Samuel 23:26)

Iram *(Ee-rahm)*
Swift; a variation of Ira. One of the clans of Edom. (Genesis 36:43)

Irijah *(Ee-ree-yah, Ear-eye-jah)*
God sees. A sentry at the gate of Jerusalem who arrests the prophet Jeremiah. (Jeremiah 37:13)

Isaac
Laughter. The son of Abraham and Sarah, born to them very late in life. One of the Hebrew patriarchs, the father of Jacob. (Genesis 17:19)

Isaiah
God is salvation. Isaiah was perhaps the most eloquent of the prophets. (Isaiah)

Ishmael
God hears. The son of Abraham and Hagar the Egyptian. (Genesis 16:11)

Israel
Wrestler with God. The name given to Jacob after he wrestled with the angel. Israel is a synonym for the Jewish people. (Genesis 32:28)

Issachar *(Iss-ah-car)*
There is a reward. The son of Jacob and Leah, one of the leaders of the 12 tribes of Israel. (Genesis 30:18)

Ittamar *(It-ah-mahr)*
Island of palm. One of Aaron's sons. (Exodus 6:23) Itmar and Ismar are variations.

Ja'azaniah, Jazaniah *(Ja-ah-zahn-ee-ah, Jah-zahn-eye-ah)*
God hears. Clan leader of the Rechabites. (Jeremiah 35:3)

Ja'aziah, Jaziah *(Jah-ah-zee-ah, Jah-zeye-ah)*
A Levite of the clan of Merari. (First Chronicles 24:26)

Jabal *(Jah-bahl)*
Lead or guide. Son of Lamech and Adah, a herdsman. (Genesis 4:20)

*There is no initial "j" sound in Hebrew so all of these names begin with "y" in the original (Jacob = Yacov). Thus, all names here may be pronounced and spelled with a "y." However, since many of these are familiar to English speakers (Jonah, James, etc.) the "j" is used with a few exceptions that either follow English usage (i.e., Yaphet) or are more melodious in the original.

Since Jah (Yah) means "God," many of these names are theophoric—referring to God.

Jacan *(Jah-kahn)*
A Gadite. (First Chronicles 5:13)

Jacob
Held by the heel, supplanter. The third of the patri-archs, Jacob fathered the 12 tribes. (Genesis 25:26). The source of the name James. (See below.)

Jaddua *(Jah-doo-ah)*
Knowledge. A Levite who returned from the Babylonian Exile. (Nehemiah 12:11)

Jadon *(Jah-dahn)*
He will judge. A volunteer in the rebuilding of Jerusalem. (Nehemiah 3:7)

Jahaziel *(Jah-hah-zee-el, or Jah-hah-zeel)*
God sees. An ally of David. (First Chronicles 12:5)

Jahdiel *(Jah-dee-el, or Jah-deel)*
God rejoices. Head of a clan. (First Chronicles 5:24)

Jahleel
Wait for god. Son of Zebulon. (Genesis 46:14)

Jahmai *(Jah-my)*
A family head. (First Chronicles 7:2)

Jair *(Jah-eer)*
To enlighten. Son of Manasseh. (Deuteronomy 3:14)

Jairus

A father who pleads with Jesus to revive his daughter. (Mark 5:22)

Jakim *(Jah-keem)*

He sets erect. A priest. (First Chronicles 24:12)

Jalam, Jalon *(Jah-lahm)*

Young man. A son of Esau and Oholibamah. (Genesis 36:5)

James

A Greek translation of Jacob, used to refer to several men in the Christian Bible, most prominently the disciple who is also associated with his brother, John. (James)

Jamin *(Jah-mean)*

Right hand. A son of Simeon, grandson of Jacob. (Genesis 46:10)

Jared

Servant. Son of Mahalael and father of Enoch. (Genesis 5:15)

Jaroah

Ben-Jaroah was a member of the tribe of Gad. (First Chronicles 5:14)

Jason

Greek form of Joshua or Jesus. An early Christian in Corinth, a contemporary of Paul. (Romans 16:21)

Javan *(Jah-vahn)*
A word that means "Greece" or "Greek." The name appears in the list of peoples who were the offspring of Noah. (Genesis 10:2)

Jazeel
God apportions. Son of Naphtali. (Genesis 46:24)

Jedaiah *(Jed-ah-yah)*
Several members of the priestly class bear this name. (First Chronicles 24:7)

Jedediah *(Jeh-deh-dee-yah, Jeh-deh-die-yah)*
Loved by God. One of the names given to King Solomon. (Second Samuel 12:25)

Jehiel *(Jeh-hee-el)*
May God live. A common biblical name held by several priests. (Second Chronicles 35:8)

Jehoadah
A descendent of Saul. (First Chronicles 8:36)

Jehosaphat
God judges. The most famous bearer of this name was a great and good king, the son of Asa and Azubah. (First Kings 22:42)

Jerahmeel
Mercy of God. A son of King Johoiakim. (Jeremiah 36:26)

Jeremiah, Jeremy

God will raise up. Jeremiah was one of the great prophets whose gloomy forcasts aroused resentment; he spent many years in jail. (Jeremiah)

Jeriah, Jerijah *(Jer-eye-ah, Jer-eye-jah)*

Foundation of God. A leader in the Levite tribe. (First Chronicles 23:19)

Jeriel *(Jer-ee-el)*

A member of the tribe of Issachar. (First Chronicles 7:2)

Jeroboam *(Jer-ah-bo-ahm)*

May the people increase. A king of Israel. (Second Kings 13:13) In Hebrew, Yeravam.

Jeroham

May he be compassionate. The father of Elkanah and grandfather of Samuel. (First Samuel 1:1)

Jesse

Gift. The grandson of Ruth and Boaz, Jesse was the father of King David, progenitor of the Messiah. (First Samuel 16:1)

Jesus

The Lord saves. (The Hebrew "Yehoshua" or "Yeshua" is rendered as "Jesus" in Greek; however, it is "Joshua" in Latin.) Jesus is called by many names in the

Christian Bible: Son of God, Son of Man, The Son, Emmanuel, even, The Name.

Jethro
Abundance, riches. Father of Zipporah and Moses' father-in-law, Jethro was a Midianite priest. (Exodus 3:1)

Jezreel
God sows. A biblical place name and also the son of the prophet Hosea. (Hosea 1:4)

Joab *(Joe-ab)*
God is Father. King David's nephew and one of his generals. (Second Samuel 8:16)

Joah
God is brother. Joah, the son of Zimnah, participated in the purification of the temple in the age of Hezekiah. (Second Chronicles 29:12)

Job
Hated, or He who turns to God. The long-suffering Job never curses the name of God, and when he intercedes on behalf of his friends, he is blessed. (Job)

Joel
God is willing. A name applied to a dozen biblical characters, Joel was one of the 12 minor prophets who preached in Judea. (Joel)

Johanan, John

God has shown favor. A very common name in both the Hebrew and Christian Bible. John is the Anglicized version applied to the disciple called The Baptist. Jesus says of John that he is not only a prophet, but the new Elijah, herald of the Messiah. (Matthew 11:9)

Jonadab

God is generous. A nephew of King David. (Second Samuel 13:3)

Jonah

Dove. Jonah was the prophet of whale fame. (Jonah)

Jonam

An ancestor of Jesus. (Luke 3:30)

Jonathan

God has given. A common biblical name, the best-known Jonathan was the son of Saul and King David's close friend. (First Samuel 14:1)

Joram

God is high. A descendant of Moses. (First Chronicles 26:25)

Jordan

Descend. In modern times, the river in ancient Palestine is used as a personal name for girls as well as boys.

Joseph
God will increase. Almost 25 percent of the Book of Genesis is devoted to the story of Joseph, the son of Jacob and Rachel. A dreamer and a shrewd politician, he married the Egyptian Asenath. (Genesis 30:24)

Joshua
The Lord is my salvation. (The Hebrew "Yehoshua" or "Yeshua" is rendered as "Joshua" in Latin. In Greek it is "Jesus.") Joshua succeeded Moses and led the Hebrews into the land of Israel. Moses changed his successor's name from Hoshua by adding a "y," one of the letters of God's name; thus, Yehoshua. (Exodus 24:13)

Josiah
God has protected. Son of Amnon, a king of Judah at the age of eight, who reigned for 31 years. (Second Kings 22:1)

Jubal
Trumpet, horn. Son of Lamech and Adah; the spiritual ancestor of all who play the lyre and the flute. (Genesis 4:21)

Judah
Praise. (Judas is the Greek form. Jude is also derived from this name.) Judah was the fourth son of Jacob and Leah and received special blessings from his father. (Genesis 29:35)

Jude
Praise. A variation of Judah, Jude was a brother of Jesus and an apostle. (Jude)

Julius
A variant of Julian which means "soft-haired" and implies youth. (Greek) A centurion who protected Paul against his enemies. (Acts 27:1)

Junias
Young lion. (Latin) A Roman Christian, a compatriot of Paul and Andronicus. (Romans 16:7)

Justus
The just one. He welcomed Paul in Corinth. (Acts 18:7)

Kadmiel *(Kahd-mee-el)*
God is before me (to the East). A Levite clan leader who returned to Judah from the Babylonian exile. (Ezra 2:40)

Kedar *(Keh-dahr)*
Swarthy. One of the sons of Ishmael. (Genesis 25:13)

Kemuel
To stand up for God. One of the sons of Nahor, who was Abraham's brother. (Genesis 22:21)

Kenan *(Keh-nahn, Kee-nin)*
To acquire or possess. A son of Enoch, and a great-grandson of Adam. (Genesis 5:9)

Kenaz *(Keh-nahz)*
Reed. A son of Elifaz and grandson of Esau. (Genesis 36:11)

Koby, Kovi
A nickname for Jacob.

Kore, Kory *(Koh-ree)*
Partridge. Kore was a Levite and gatekeeper. (First Chronicles 9:19)

Laban *(Lah-bahn)*
White. (In Hebrew, pronounced Lah-vahn.) Rebecca's brother and the father of matriarchs Rachel and Leah, thus grandfather of the 12 tribes of Israel. (Genesis 28:5)

Ladan *(Lah-dahn)*
Witness. A member of the tribe of Ephraim. (First Chronicles 7:26)

Lael *(Lay-el)*
Belonging to God. A member of the house of Gershon. (Numbers 3:24)

Lazarus
God has given help. (Greek, from the Hebrew Elazar) Lazarus of Bethany, brother of Martha and Mary, died and was restored to life by Jesus. (John 11:1–5)

Lemuel
Who belongs to God. An alternate name for Solomon, to whom Proverbs 31 is attributed. Lem is a pet name.

Levi
Attendant upon. The third of Jacob's sons born to Leah. His descendants became the Levites, the priests of the Temple. (Genesis 29:34) Lev is a diminutive.

Linus
Flax-colored. A Roman Christian. (Second Timothy 4:21)

Lotan *(Low-tahn)*
To envelop. Son of Seir the Horite. (Genesis 36:20)

Lucius
Light. (Latin) A contemporary of Paul, an early Christian in Corinth. (Romans 16:21)

Luke
An Anglicization of Lucius. Luke was one of the apostles, a physician who worked with Paul. (Luke)

Machir *(Mah-keer)*
Goods. A son of Manasseh, grandson of Jacob. (Genesis 50:23)

Maharai *(Mah-har-eye, Mah-har-ee)*
Haste. One of King David's warriors. (Second Samuel 23:28)

Malachi
Messenger or angel. The last of the prophets. (Malachi)

Malkam
God is their King. A member of the tribe of Benjamin. (First Chronicles 8:9)

Manasseh, Menasseh
Causing to forget. Joseph's son, born in Egypt. (Genesis 41:51)

Manoah
Place of rest. Father of Samson. (Judges 13:2)

Mark
Hammer. (Latin) One of the Apostles. A son of Mary, cousin of Barnabas, companion of Paul and Peter. (Mark)

Mattan
Gift. An ancestor of Jesus. (Matthew 1:15)

Mattaniah, Mattanya
Gift of God. A common biblical name which belonged to King Zedekiah before he ascended the throne. (Second Kings 24:17)

Mattathias
Gift from God. (The Greek form of Matityahu) A common biblical name, Mattathias was the father of Judah Maccabee, the patriarch of the Hasmonean dynasty. (First Maccabees 2:1) Also listed as an ancestor of Jesus. (Luke 3:25)

Matthew
Gift (Greek derivation of the Hebrew Mattaniah or Mattathius/Matityahu) One of the 12 apostles. (Matthew)

Matthias
An abbreviated form of Mattathias. A disciple chosen to take the place of Judas Iscariot and complete the group of 12 apostles. (Acts 1:23)

Menachem *(Meh-nah-hem)*
Comforter. A biblical king. (Second Kings 15:14)

Meshach *(Mee-shak)*
A name given to Daniel's companion, Mishael, by King

Nebuchadnezzar. (Daniel 1:7) Meshach, with Shadrach and Abednigo, survived terrible trials for his faith.

Micah *(My-kah)*
Who is like God. Micah (a shortened form of Michael) appears many times as a biblical name; the most famous was a prophet in Judah who denounced oppression by the ruling classes. (Micah)

Michael
Who is like God. Several Michaels appear in the Bible; especially the angel closest to God, and God's messenger who carried out divine judgments. In the Book of Daniel (12:1), he is called "the prince." Variations on Michael include Mike, Mickey, Mitchell, and the Russian, Misha.

Midian *(Mih-dee-un)*
Strife. A son of Abraham and Keturah. (Genesis 25:2) Also a place name.

Mishael *(Mee-sha-el)*
Borrowed. An uncle of Moses and Aaron. (Exodus 6:22)

Misham *(Mee-shahm)*
To cleanse. (Assyrian) A Benjaminite. (First Chronicles 8:12)

Mordecai *(Mor-deh-kye)*
Warrior or warlike. (Persian) Queen Esther's cousin who helped save the Jews of Shushan. (Esther 2:7)

Moses
Because I drew him out of the water. (Son or child in Egyptian.) The leader who brought the Israelites out of bondage in Egypt. (Exodus 2:10)

Naaman *(Nah-mahn, Nay-man)*
Sweet, beautiful. A general in the army of Aram who was cured of leprosy by the prophet Elisha. (Second Kings 5:1)

Nadav, Nedav *(Nah-dahv)*
Benefactor. Eldest son of Aaron. (Exodus 6:23) Also spelled Nadab.

Naham *(Nah-hahm)*
Comforter. Brother of Hodiah. (First Chronicles 4:19)

Nahum *(Nah-hoom)*
Comforted. One of the minor prophets (Nahum); also listed as an ancestor of Jesus. (Luke 3:25)

Naphtali, Naftali

To wrestle. Jacob's sixth son by Bilhah. (Genesis 30:8)
Tali is a nickname.

Nathan

God has given. Nathan was one of the minor prophets
who anointed Solomon king. (Second Samuel 5:14) In
Hebrew, Natan *(Naht-ahn)*.

Nathaniel

Gift of God. Nathaniel was David's brother. (First
Chronicles 2:14) Also one of the first disciples of Jesus.
(John 21:2)

Nedabiah *(Ned-ah-bee-yah, Ned-ah-buy-ah)*

God's gift. A descendent of Solomon. (First Chronicles
3:18)

Nehemiah *(Neh-hem-yah, Nee-hem-my-ah)*

Comforted of the Lord. A governor of Judea who
helped rebuild the walls of Jerusalem. (Ezra 2:2)

Nemuel

Industrious. (From the Hebrew for "ant.") Of the tribe
of Reuben. (Numbers 26:9)

Nereus *(Ner-ee-us)*

A Christian of Rome. (Romans 16:15)

Nicanor
Victory. (Greek) One of the seven assistants to the disciples of Jesus. (Acts 6:5)

Nicholas
Victory of the people. (Greek) A follower of Jesus from Antioch. One of the seven assistants to the disciples of Jesus. (Acts 6:5)

Nicodemus *(Nik-oh-dee-mus)*
Victory of the people. (Greek) A defender of Jesus. (John 3:1)

Noadiah *(Noh-ah-die-ah)*
Assembly of God. A Levite. (Ezra 8:33)

Noah
Rest, quiet. Noah, the only righteous man of his time, was selected to survive the great flood sent by God to punish an evil world. (Genesis 5:29)

Noam
Sweetness, friendship. A variation of Naaman.

Obadiah, Ovadiah
Servant of God. A common name in the Hebrew Bible, Obadiah was one of the 12 minor prophets. (Obadiah)

Ofir *(Oh-fear)*
Gold. Son of Yaktan. (Genesis 10:29)

Omar
Eloquent. Son of Eliphaz. (Genesis 36:11)

Omri *(Ohm-ree)*
My sheaf. A king in Israel. (First Kings 16:16)

Oren, Orrin
Fir tree, cedar. A descendant of Judah. (First Chronicles 2:25)

Orev
Raven. A Midianite leader. (Judges 7:25)

Oved
Servant. The son of Ruth and Boaz and King David's grandfather. (Ruth 4:17)

Ozni *(Ohz-nee)*
Strength, hearing. Son of Gad, grandson of Jacob. (Numbers 26:16)

Paul
Greek version of Saul, "asked for." The great missionary disciple whose theology informs much of the

Christian Bible. The "Acts of the Apostles" are chiefly the acts of Paul.

Peter
Rock. (Greek, translated from the Aramaic "Cephas") The "first" of the 12 apostles, who is given the name of Peter as foundation of the church. (Matthew 16:18)

Philemon
Beloved. (Greek) A Christian of Colossea. (Philemon 1)

Philip
Friend of horses. (Greek) One of the 12 disciples who brings Nathaniel to Jesus. (John 1:43) Philip the evangelist is also listed as one of the seven assistants to the disciples. (Acts 6:5)

Phineas
Black. Son of Eleazar and grandson of Aaron. (Exodus 6:25) An Anglicized version of the Hebrew Pinchas *(Pin-hahs)*.

Raham *(Rah-hahm)*
Compassion. A descendant of Judah. (First Chronicles 2:44) Raheem is the Aramaic version.

Ram
Exalted, mighty. A descendant of Judah. (First Chronicles 2:25)

Rami *(Rah-mee, Ray-mee)*
Mane or crest. Rami is a version of Rama *(Rah-mah)*, a grandson of Noah. (Genesis 10:7)

Raphael
God has healed. A temple gatekeeper. (First Chronicles 26:7) An archangel who appears in the apocryphal book of Tobit. (Tobit 3:17) Rafi and Rafe are nicknames.

Reuben, Reuven
Behold, a son. Jacob and Leah's firstborn. (Genesis 30:32)

Rimon *(Ree-moan)*
Pomegranate. A biblical place name and the father of two of King Saul's officers. (Second Samuel 4:2)

Ron
Joy or song.

Rufus
Red. (Greek) A Christian of Rome. (Romans 16:13)

Samson

Service, ministry. The strong man was actually one of the judges of Israel, but most famous for his betrayal by Delilah. (Judges 13:24)

Samuel

His name is God. Samuel, the son of Hannah, was a prophet and judge who anointed King Saul as first king of Israel. (First and Second Samuel)

Saul

Borrowed. Saul was the first king of Israel, from the tribe of Benjamin. (First Samuel 9:2)

Seth

Appointed. Adam and Eve's son, born after Abel's death. (Genesis 4:25) In Hebrew, Shet.

Shadrach

A name given to Daniel's companion, Hananiah, by King Nebuchadnezzar. (Daniel 1:7) Shadrach, with Meshach and Abednigo, survived terrible trials for his faith.

Shem

Name. Eldest son of Noah. (Genesis 5:32)

Shilo, Shiloh

The gift is God's. A biblical place name (Joshua 21:2) and also a reference to the Messiah. (Genesis 49:10)

Silas

Borrowed. (Greek form of Saul.) A Roman Christian and a leader among Christians in Jerusalem. (Acts 15:22)

Simon

To hear or be heard. The second son born to Jacob and Leah. (Genesis 29:33) Simon is the Greek version, Simeon the Anglicized; the Hebrew is pronounced *Shih-moan*. There are many Simons in the Christian Bible, one a brother of Jesus. (Matthew 13:55)

Solomon

Peace. The son of David and Bathsheba, he rebuilt the Temple and wrote Song of Songs, Proverbs, and Ecclesiastes. His reputation for wisdom is enshrined in the word "solomonic." (Second Samuel 12:24)

Stephen

Crown. One of the seven assistants to the disciples, called "deacons" in Greek. He is called "a man full of faith and of the Holy Ghost." (Acts 6:5)

Tahan *(Tah-hahn)*
A son of Ephraim. (First Chronicles 7:25)

Tal, Tali, Talor *(Tahl, Tah-lee, Tah-loar)*
Dew, my dew, dew of light. Tali is a nickname for Naftali, also used as a girl's name.

Tamir *(Tah-meer)*
Tall. Like the "tamar" or palm tree.

Tavor, Tabor *(Tah-voar, Tay-boar)*
A place name, a mountain south of the Galilee. (Judges 4:6)

Temani *(Teh-mah-nee)*
One who comes from the south. A member of tribe of Judah. (First Chronicles 4:6)

Terah
Wild goat. The father of Abraham. (Genesis 11:25)

Tertius
Third. (Latin) Paul's secretary. (Romans 16:22)

Thaddeus
Gift of God. (Greek) One of the 12 disciples. (Matthew 10:3)

Theodosius, Theodotus
Given by God. (Greek) A messenger sent by Nicanor

to the Jews. (Second Maccabees 14:19)

Theophilus
Friend of God. (Greek) The person to whom Luke addressed his writings. (Luke 1:3)

Thomas
Twin. (Greek) One of the twelve apostles who is famous for believing only what he saw. (John 20:24)

Tilon
Small mound. A descendant of Judah. (First Chronicles 4:20)

Timon
One of the seven assistants to the disciples of Jesus. (Acts 6:5)

Timothy
Who honors God. (Greek) A disciple and a companion of Paul. (First and Second Timothy)

Tiras *(Tie-rus)*
One of the sons of Japhet. (Genesis 10:2)

Tiria, Tirya *(Teer-ee-yah, Teer-yah)*
To be awake. (Aramaic) A member of the tribe of Judah. (First Chronicles 4:16)

Titus
Size or power. (Latin. Titos in Greek.) A Christian of pagan origin who assists Paul. (Titus)

Tobiah, Tobias

God is good. The son of Tobit in the apocryphal Book of Tobit. Toby is a popular nickname.

Uri *(Oo-ree, Yoo-ree)*

My light. Father of Bezalel, the artist. (Exodus 31:2)

Uriah *(Oo-ree-ah, You-rye-uh)*

God is my light. Bathsheba's first husband. (Second Samuel 11:3)

Uriel *(Oo-ree-el, You-ree-el)*

God is my light. A Levite in the time of David. (First Chronicles 15:5) One of the four angels who reside around God's throne.

Uzziah *(Oo-zee-ah, You-zeye-ah)*

God is my strength. One of David's champions. (First Chronicles 11:44)

Uzziel *(Oo-zee-el, You-zee-el)*

God is my strength. A common biblical name; the first one mentioned was a grandson of Levi. (Exodus 6:18)

Yadon *(Yah-doan)*
He will judge. A supporter of Nehemiah. (Nehemiah 3:7)

Yair *(Yah-eer)*
To light up. A grandson of Joseph, son of Manasseh. (Deuteronomy 3:14)

Yakim *(Yah-keem)*
A shortened form of Yehoyakim. (Jehoiakim, "God will establish.") A priest in the time of King David. (First Chronicles 24:12)

Yalon *(Yah-loan)*
He will rest. A son of Caleb. (First Chronicles 4:17)

Yanai *(Yahn-eye)*
To shake, wave, or answer. A descendant of Gad. (First Chronicles 5:12)

Yared *(Yah-rehd)*
To descend. The grandfather of Methuselah. (Genesis 5:15)

*Although there are many names that begin with the "y" sound in Hebrew, many of these are familiar as "j" names in English (i.e., Jacob = Yacov) and most are found under "j" in this book (Jonah, James, Jesus, etc.). The names here either follow English usage (i.e., Yaphet) or are simply more melodious with the original "y" sound. Since Jah (Yah) means "God," many of these names are theophoric—referring to God.

Yaval *(Yah-vahl)*
Stream. Son of Lemach and Adah. (Genesis 4:20)
Jubal, in English.

Yavin *(Yah-veen)*
One who is intelligent. A Canaanite king in the time of
Deborah. (Joshua 11:1)

Yefet *(Yeh-phet)*
Beautiful. Also spelled Yephet, Yafet, Yaphet. Yefet was
one of Noah's sons. (Genesis 5:32)

Yefune, Yefuneh *(Yeh-foo-neh)*
To face or turn. The father of Caleb. (Numbers 13:6)

Yehiel *(Yeh-hee-el, Yeh-heel)*
May God live. Yehiel was chief musician in the court of
King David. (Ezra 8:9)

Yigal *(Yee-gahl)*
He will redeem. One of the scouts sent by Moses to
explore the Promised Land. (Numbers 13:7)

Yitran *(Yeet-rahn)*
Excellence. A member of the tribe of Asher. (First
Chronicles 7:37)

Yotam *(Yo-tahm)*
God is perfect. One of Gideon's sons. (Judges 9:5)

Zakai *(Zahk-eye)*
Pure, clean. The head of a family of returnees from the Babylonian exile. (Ezra 2:9)

Zan, Zane
Nourished. A kind of plant mentioned in the Bible. (Second Chronicles 16:14)

Zanoah
A place name. A town in Judah. (Joshua 15:34)

Zavad *(Za-vahd)*
Gift. An officer in David's army. (First Chronicles 11:41)

Zavdi, Zavdiel *(Zahv-dee, Zahv-dee-el)*
My gift, gift of God. A descendant of Benjamin. (First Chronicles 8:19)

Zebadiah
Gift of God. There are several in the Bible; one was a Benjamanite who lived in Jerusalem. (First Chronicles 8:15)

Zebulon, Zevulon
To exalt or honor. The sixth son of Jacob and Leah. (Genesis 30:20)

Zechariah

Remember the Lord. The name of one of the minor prophets, and of many others in the Bible, including a king of Israel. (Second Kings 14:29) In English, this name is often spelled Zachariah. Zachary is an abbreviated form.

Zedekiah

God is righteousness. The last king of Judah, who changed his name from Mattaniah. (Second Kings 24:17)

Zephaniah

God has treasured. A seventh-century prophet who belonged to the family of Judah. (Zephaniah)

Zerach *(Zer-ahk)*

Light or shine. The son of Judah and Tamar. (Genesis 38:30)

Zerachiah

Light of the Lord. A son of Pinchas. (Ezra 7:4)

Zimran *(Zim-rahn)*

Goat, sacred thing, or my vine. Son of Abraham and Keturah. (Genesis 25:2)

Zuriel

God is my rock. Head of a Merari clan family. (Numbers 3:35)

A Daughter! Bible Names for Girls

Aarona, Arona *(Ah-hah-roan-ah, Ah-roan-ah)*
Teaching or singing. Feminine version of Aaron.

Abigail

Father's joy. King David's wife was known for her
beauty, wisdom, and powers of prophecy. (1 Samuel
25:3)

Abira *(Ah-bee-rah)*
Strong.

Abra *(Ah-brah)*
A diminutive of Abraham.

Adah, Ada
Ornament. The first wife of Lamech and mother of Jabal and Jubal. (Genesis 36:2)

Adena, Adina *(Ah-dee-nah)*
Noble or adorned, gentle.

Adira *(Ah-dee-rah)*
Strong or mighty.

Adra
Glory or majesty. (Aramaic)

Ahava *(Ah-hah-vah)*
Love, beloved. Also a town and river in Babylon. (Ezra 8:15)

Amira *(Ah-mee-rah)*
Speech, or ear of corn.

Anah, Anat *(Ah-naht)*
To sing. (Spring, in ancient Ugaritic) Mother of Shamgar (Genesis 36:2); also the name of a Semitic goddess (Judges 3:31).

Anna, Ann
The Greek form of the Hebrew Hanna, and the source of many diminutives: Annette, Annie, Anita, Anya.

Antonia
A biblical place name. A fortress built by Herod. (Second Maccabees 4:12)

Arella
Angel, messenger.

Ariella
Lioness of god. Feminine version of Ariel.

Armona
Castle or palace.

Arna
Cedar.

Arnona
Roaring stream. Feminine of Arnon.

Arza
Cedar beams.

Asenat *(Ah-se-naht)*
Belonging to the goddess Neith. (Egyptian. "Thornbush" in Aramaic.) The wife of Joseph and mother of Ephraim and Mannaseh. (Genesis 41:45)

Ashira *(Ah-sheer-ah)*
Wealthy.

Asia
This place name appears in the Bible several times, though it refers to different locations depending upon where it is used. In writing to the Corinthians, Paul sends greetings to the church of Asia. (First Corinthians 16:19)

Atalia, Atalya *(Ah-tahl-yah)*
God is exalted. The daughter of King Omri, mother of King Ahaziah. (Second Kings 8:26)

Atara, Atarah *(Ah-tah-rah)*
Crown. One of the wives of Jerahmeel, mother of Onam. (First Chronicles 2:26)

Atira *(Ah-teer-ah)*
Prayer.

Avital *(Ah-vee-tahl)*
Dew of my father. Avital was one of King David's wives. (Second Samuel 3:4)

Aviva *(Ah-vee-vah)*
Spring.

Aviya, Avia, Aviah *(Ah-vee-yah)*
God is my father. The mother of Hezekiah, a king of Judah. (Second Chronicles 29:1)

Avna *(Ahv-nah)*
A lake or river in Syria. (Second Kings 5:12)

Aya, Ayah *(Ah-yah)*
To fly swiftly. The name of a bird of prey. A masculine name in the Bible, a descendant of Esau. (Genesis 36:24)

Ayala *(Ah-yah-lah)*
Deer or gazelle.

Aza, Azah, Aziza *(A-zah, Ah-zee-zah)*
Strong.

Azariah *(Ah-zar-ee-ah, Ah-zar-yah)*
God has helped. A masculine name in the Bible. (First Chronicles 2:8)

Azriella *(Ahz-ree-el-ah)*
God is my strength. Feminine of Azriel.

Azubah *(Ah-zoo-bah)*
Forsaken. The mother of King Jehosaphat of Judah. (First Kings 22:42)

Ba'ara *(Bah-ah-rah)*
To burn or consume. (Aramaic) The wife of one of Benjamin's sons. (First Chronicles 8:8)

Bakura, Bikurah *(Bah-koo-rah, Bih-koo-rah)*

Ripe, usually referring to figs.

Batsheva *(Baht-sheh-vah)*

Daughter of the oath. The beautiful Batsheva *(Bath-shee-bah* to most English-speakers) was one of King David's wives and the mother of King Solomon. (Second Samuel 11:3)

Benjamina

The feminine form of Benjamin. Binyamina would be the Hebrew pronunciation.

Beri

My well. A masculine name in the Bible. (Hosea 1:1)

Berit *(Beh-reet)*

Well, a source of water.

Bernice, Berenice

Bringer of victory. Herod's daughter, who was present when Paul appeared before her brother, Agrippa. (Acts 25:13) Beronica is a variant form.

Bet, Beth

Beth is a common prefix that means "house of" and is associated with many place names in the bible, such as Beth-Eden, Beth-Barath, and Beth-Biri.

Bethany
A Greek and Latin version of "house of figs." A town on the eastern slopes of the Mount of Olives, the place where Jesus raised Lazarus from the dead and where, according to Luke, the ascension took place. (John 11:18)

Bilhah *(Beel-hah)*
Weak or old. Maidservant of Jacob's wife, Rachel, and the mother of two tribes of Israel: Dan and Naftali. (Genesis 30:3)

Bina *(Bee-nah)*
Understanding, intelligence.

Bira *(Bee-rah)*
Capital.

Bitya, Bitia *(Bit-yah, Bit-tee-yah)*
Daughter of God. A daughter of Pharoah who married Mered, of the tribe of Judah. (First Chronicles 4:18)

Basmat *(Bahz-maht)*
Perfumed. (Aramaic) A wife of Esau (Genesis 26:34) and also a daughter of King Solomon (First Kings 4:15).

Carmel, Carmelle, Carmela

Vineyard. A mountain overlooking the plain of Jezreel, and also a town in the highlands of Judah. (Joshua 19:26) Carmiya means "vineyard of the Lord."

Chloe

Blooming or verdant. (Greek) Paul meets a group of people "of the house of Chloe." (First Corinthians 1:11)

Claudia

From Claudius. (Lame in Greek) A Christian woman of Rome. (Second Timothy 4:21)

Cornelia

Feminine version of Cornelius.

Cyrene

A city in North Africa, from which early Christians were among the founders of the Church of Antioch in Syria. (First Maccabees 15:23)

---

* Many Hebrew names begin with a guttural Hebrew "ch" sound that is not used in English. These tend to be Anglicized to "h."

Dalia, Dalya
Branch.

Damaris
Gentle girl. (Greek) An Athenian woman who converted to Christianity. (Acts 17:34)

Daniella, Danielle
God is my judge. The feminine version of Daniel. Also Dania, Dani, Danya.

Dannah
Fortress. A place name, a town in the highlands of Judah. (Joshua 15:49)

Danya
Feminine of Dan.

Daphne, Dafna
Laurel. (Greek) A place name, near Antioch in Syria, famous for its temple to Apollo. (Second Maccabees 4:33)

Dara
Pearl or marble. A man's name in the Bible, one of the sons of Zerah. (First Chronicles 2:6)

Darona, Dorona
Gift.

Davida, Davita

The feminine of David, meaning beloved or friend.

Deborah, Debra, Devorah, Devra

To speak kind words, or a swarm of bees. There are three Deborahs in the Bible, the most famous being the prophetess and judge who led a revolt against a Canaanite king. (Judges 4:4)

Delilah

Coquette. (Old Arabic) Samson's lover who betrays him to the Phillistines. (Judges 16:4)

Derora, Drora

Freedom.

Diana

Divine. (Latin. Roman goddess of the moon.) The Greek goddess, whose name appears in a story in which Paul preaches against false gods. (Acts 19:23–40)

Dimona, Divona

South.

Dina, Dinah, Deena, Dena

Judgment. Dinah was the daughter of Leah and Jacob—the only girl among his children. (Genesis 34:3)

Dinia, Dinya

Judgment of the Lord.

Dorcas
Gazelle. (Greek. Ophrah in Hebrew, Tabitha in Aramaic.) A Christian woman of Jaffa known for her charitable work; she was resurrected by Paul. (Acts 9:36)

Dorit *(Dor-eet)*
Generation.

Dorya
Generation of God.

Drusilla
A daughter of Herod Agrippa I, who hears Paul's address about faith. (Acts 24:24)

Eden
Delight. The original home of Adam and Eve and also a personal name, albeit a man's; a Levite in the time of King Hezekiah. (Second Chronicles 31:15)

Edna
Delight, pleasure. Edna, mother of Sarah and mother-in-law of Tobia, is a character in the book of Tobit. (7:2)

Efrat *(Eff-raht)*
Honored, distinguished. The wife of Caleb. (First Chronicles 2:19) Also, Efrata.

Efrona
Songbird.

Elana
Oak tree. Also spelled Elona, Ilona, or Ilana.

Eliana
God has answered me. Also Elaine, Elianna.

Eliava, Eliavah *(El-ee-ah-vah)*
My God is willing.

Elinoar
God of my youth.

Eliora *(El-ee-oar-ah)*
God is my light.

Elisheva *(El-ee-sheh-vah)*
God is my oath. Elisheva was Aaron's wife and thus the matriarch of the priestly caste. (Exodus 6:23) Several women named Elisheva/Elizabeth (Greek) appear in the Christian Bible including the mother of John the Baptist. (Luke 1:24) Elizabeth has many nicknames, among them: Ella, Elisa, Eliza, Elise, Elsie, Betsy, Liz, Libby, Bette, Beth, Betty, and Elyssa.

Eliya *(El-ee-yah)*
The Lord is my God. Feminine form of Elijah.

Elza
Joy.

Emanuella
God is with us. Feminine version of Emmanuel.

Esther
Star. (Persian) The heroine of the story of Purim, who, with help from her cousin Mordechai, averted the annihilation of the Jews of Persia. The Hebrew name for Esther is Hadassah, which means myrtle. Variations include Esta, Estelle, and Estella. (Esther)

Etana *(Eh-tahn-ah)*
Strong. Feminine version of Ethan—Etan in Hebrew.

Eunice
Fine victory. (Greek) An early Christian, the mother of Timothy. (Acts 16:1)

Eve
Life. In Genesis, Eve is the first woman, the mother of all human life. (Genesis 4:1) In Hebrew, Hava.

Ezriella *(Ez-ree-ella)*
God is my help. The feminine for Ezra.

Gabriella, Gavriella

God is my strength. The feminine version of Gabriel. Nicknames include Gabbie and Ella.

Gali, Galit *(Gah-lee, Gah-leet)*

Fountain or spring.

Galya**

Hill of God.

Gamliela, Gamlielle

God is my reward. Feminine forms of Gamliel.

Ganit *(Gah-neet)*

Defender.

Ganya

Garden of the Lord. Gania is an alternate spelling.

Gavrilla

Heroine, strong. A variation on Gabriella.

Gayora

Valley of light.

Except where noted, these names all begin with a hard "g," as in "good." The soft "g," as in "Georgia," is an Anglicization.

** The suffix "ya" adds God to the name.

Geona
Exhaltation or wisdom.

Giah *(Gee-ah)*
Bubbling. Place name, near Gibeon. (Second Samuel 2:24) The "g" is soft.

Gila *(Gee-lah)*
Joy. Gilana and Gilat also mean joy. Gilia or Giliya means "My joy is in the Lord."

Gilada
My joy is forever.

Gina, Ginat
Garden. Ginat is a man's name in the Bible. (First Kings 16:21) (Hard "g" in Hebrew, soft "g" in English)

Giora *(Gee-oh-rah)*
Stranger.

Giva, Givona
Hill.

Hadara, Hadura *(Hah-dah-rah, Hah-dur-ah)*
Splendid. Feminine version of Hadar.

Hadass, Hadassah

Myrtle tree, a symbol of victory. This is the Hebrew form of the name Esther. (Book of Esther)

Hagar *(Hah-gahr)*

Stranger. The Egyptian servant of Sarah who at her mistress's request gave Abraham a son, Ishmael. (Genesis 16:1)

Hali

A place name, a town south of Aphek. (Joshua 19:25)

Hamuda *(Hah-moo-dah)*

Precious.

Hannah

Gracious, merciful. The wife of Elkanan, mother of Samuel, and the subject of a tale of infertility and faith rewarded. (First Samuel 1:1) Another Anna/Hannah welcomes the child Jesus to the temple (Luke 2:36). The Anglicized Anna and all its derivations (Anne, Annette, Anita) are rooted in this name.

Hasia *(Hah-see-yah)*

Protected of the Lord.

Hasida *(Hah-see-dah)*

Pious one. Also, stork.

Haviva *(Hah-vee-vah)*

Beloved.

Hedia, Hedya
Voice of the Lord.

Hedva
Joy.

Hefziba
My desire. Mother of King Manasseh and wife of King Hezekiah. (Second Kings 21:1)

Helah *(Heh-lah, Hah-lay)*
Rust. One of the wives of Ashur. (First Chronicles 4:5)

Hemda
Precious.

Hilla
Praise.

Hodia, Hodiya
Praise the Lord. Sister of Nahum, also a man's name. (First Chronicles 4:10)

Hulda
To dig. A prophetess consulted by Josiah. (Second Kings 22:14)

Ilana
Oak tree. Also spelled Elana.

Imnah
Good fortune. A man's name in the Bible. Son of Asher. (Genesis 46:17)

Irit *(Ear-eet)*
Daffodil.

Isaaca *(Ee-sah-kah)*
Laughter. The feminine of Isaac.

Isca
Annointed. A daughter of Haran, brother of Abraham. (Genesis 11:29)

Iti, Itti *(It-tee)*
With me.

Itiya, Itia *(It-tee-yah)*
God is with me.

Jacoba
To supplant. The feminine of Jacob.

Jaime, Jaimee, Jamie
Variations on James.

Jasmine, Jasmina
Persian flower name.

Jedidah *(Jeh-dee-dah, Jeh-die-dah)*
Beloved. Mother of King Josiah. (Second Kings 22:1)

Jemima *(Jeh-mee-mah)*
Dove. A daughter of Job. (Job 42:14)

Jemina *(Jeh-mee-nah)*
Righthanded, signifying strength.

Jerusha
Inheritance. The wife of King Uziah of Judah and the daughter of Zadok. (Second Kings 15:33)

* There is no initial "j" sound in Hebrew. These names begin with "y" in the original (Jacoba = Yacova). Thus, all names in this section may be pronounced and spelled with a "y." However, since many of these are familiar to English speakers (Judith, Julia, etc.) the "j" is used with a few exceptions that either follow English usage (i.e., Yael) or are more melodious with the original.

Many of these names are theophoric since Jah (Yah) means "God."

Jessie, Jessica, Jessamine
God's gift. Variations on the masculine Jesse.

Joanna, Joanne
God has shown favor. (Greek version from Yohanan) One of the women who accompanies Jesus, and later announces the resurrection. (Luke 8:3, Luke 24:10)

Joelle, Joella
God is willing. Feminine version of Joel.

Johanna
God is gracious. Feminine of Jochanon.

Jonatha
God has given. Feminine for Jonathan.

Jonina *(Joe-nee-nah)*
A dove. Feminine of Jonah.

Jordan, Jordana
The largest river in Israel; to descend. Jordi, Jordie are diminutives.

Josepha, Josette
God will increase. Feminine versions of Joseph. Also Josephine, Josefina.

Judith
Praise. In the Apocryphal story, Judith was the heroine who saved Jerusalem by pretending to defect to

General Holofernes' camp, where she beheaded him while he slept. (Judith)

Julia
Feminine form of Julian. A Christian woman of Rome. (Romans 16:15)

Kadia, Kadya *(Kah-dee-yah, Kahd-yah)*
Pitcher.

Kanara, Kanera
Songbird.

Karmil *(Kahr-meel)*
Red, crimson.

Karna
Horn, as in ram's horn.

Katania, Katanya
Small. Feminine version of Hakatan, a returnee from the Babylonian exile. (Ezra 8:12) Ketana and Ketina are variations.

Keliah, Kelita *(Keh-lee-yah, Keh-lee-tah)*
A Levite in the time of Ezra. A man's name. (Ezra 10:23)

Kelila *(Keh-lee-lah)*
Crown or laurel. Kayla and Kyla are variations.

Keren
Horn.

Ketura *(Keh-too-rah)*
Perfumed. Abraham's wife after Sarah's death. (Genesis 25:1)

Kezia, Keziah
Fragrant. One of Job's daughters. (Job 42:14) Also spelled Cassia.

Kinneret
Lyre or harp. The Hebrew name of the Sea of Galilee.

Kirya
Village. Also spelled Kiria.

Kitra
Crown.

Kohava
Star.

Kolia, Kolya *(Ko-lee-yah, Koal-yah)*
God's voice.

Laila, Layla
Night.

Latifa
Caress.

Leah *(Lay-ah, Lee-ah)*
Weariness. (Mistress or ruler in Assyrian.) Jacob's first wife, Leah gave birth to six sons and a daughter. (Genesis 29:16) Also spelled Lea, Leia, Lia.

Leora, Liora *(Lee-oh-rah)*
My light.

Levana, Livana
Moon, or white. A man's name in the Bible—one who returned from the Babylonian exile. (Ezra 2:45) Other versions include Levona and Livona.

Levia, Leviah *(Lev-yah, Lev-ee-ah)*
Lioness of the Lord. The feminine form of Levi.

Levona
Frankincense.

Lila
She is mine. Also Persian for lilac.

Lilith
An Akkadian name for a female demon; according to legend, Adam's wife before Eve. (Isaiah 34:14)

Lirona *(Lee-roan-ah)*
My song.

Livia, Livya
Crown. When the accent falls on the last syllable, Livia means lioness.

Lois
Good. (Greek) The grandmother of Timothy. (Second Timothy 1:5)

Luza
Almond tree. Luz is the ancient name of the biblical town, Beth El.

Lydia
Cultured. (Greek) An early convert to Christianity and friend to Paul. (Acts 16:14)

Madya
Delight of God. A man's name in the Bible, a priest who returned from the Babylonian exile. (Nehemiah 12:5)

Magdalena, Magdalene

Magdala was a town on the shore of the Galilee. Magdalene means "of or from Magdala." Mary Magdalene was healed by Jesus (Luke 8:2) and was the first to see Jesus risen (John 20:11). Madeleine is a variation.

Mahalat

Praise. One biblical Mahalat was a daughter of Ishmael; another was a granddaughter of King David. (First Chronicles 11:18)

Mahira, Mehira *(Mah-hee-rah)*

Energetic.

Mahlah

Ample. A daughter of Zelophehad. (Numbers 36:11)

Mahli *(Mah-lee)*

A man's name. A grandson of Levi. (Exodus 6:19)

Malka

Queen.

Malkiah, Malkiya *(Mahl-kee-yah)*

Queen of God.

Mara

Bitter. The name Naomi takes upon herself in sorrow. (Ruth 1:20)

Margalit *(Mar-gah-leet)*
Pearl.

Marni, Marnina
Rejoice.

Martha
Mistress. (Aramaic) The sister of Mary and Lazarus of Bethany. She acknowledges Jesus as Messiah. (John 11:1)

Marva
Plant in the mint family.

Mary
Lady. The name is derived from the Hebrew Miriam (Miryam). The wife of Joseph and mother of Jesus is but one of several important Marys in the Christian Bible: i.e., Mary, the sister of Lazarus; Mary Magdalene; Mary, mother of James and Joseph. Mary has given rise to dozens of variations, including Maria, Mari, Marie, Mariel, Mariele, Marion, Marya, Maura, Maureen, Minnie, Moira, Molly.

Matanya
Gift of God. The given name of King Zedekiah. (Second Kings 24:17)

Mayana *(My-ahn-ah)*
Fountain, spring.

Mehetabel
God does good. Daughter of Matred. (First Chronicles 1:50)

Meira, Mira, Myra *(My-rah)*
Light. Myra is a city in Lycia. (Acts 27:5)

Meona *(Mee-oh-nah)*
Dwelling place, referring especially to the ancient Temple.

Merab, Merav *(Mehr-ahb)*
Daughter of Saul. (First Samuel 18:19)

Meraiah *(Mer-eye-ah)*
Loved by God. Masculine name; head of a priestly family. (Nehemiah 12:12)

Merari *(Meh-rahr-ee)*
Beloved. (Egyptian) Masculine name; a son of Levi. (Genesis 46:11)

Mesha *(Mee-sha)*
Saved, freed. Masculine name; a Benjaminite family chief. (First Chronicles 8:9)

Michaela
Who is like God? Feminine of Michael, one of the archangels. Mia is a nickname.

Michal *(Mee-hal)*

A contraction of Michaela. Michal was King Saul's youngest daughter and one of King David's wives. (Second Samuel 6:23)

Milcah

Queen. (Akin to Malka.) Abraham's sister-in-law. (Genesis 11:29)

Mishael *(Mee-sha-el)*

Borrowed. A man's name. (Exodus 6:22)

Miriam, Miryam

Sorrow or bitterness. ("Mistress of the sea" in Chaldean.) Miriam was a prophetess, singer, and dancer, the sister of Moses and Aaron. (Exodus 15:20) This is the source of the name Mary. Nicknames for Miriam include Mindy, Minna, Mira, and Mollie.

Moriah

Teacher. Also the mountain of Isaac's sacrifice.

Moriel, Morielle *(Mor-ee-el)*

God is my teacher.

Naamah *(Nah-ah-mah, Nah-mah)*
Gracious, beautiful. Mother of King Rehoboam. (First Kings 14:21)

Naarah *(Nah-ah-rah, Nah-rah)*
Young girl. One of the wives of Judah. (First Chronicles 4:5)

Nadavya *(Nah-dahv-yah)*
Generous, noble. Feminine form of Nadav.

Naomi
Beautiful, pleasant. Ruth's mother-in-law. (Ruth 1:2)

Nasia, Nasya *(Nah-see-yah, Nas-yah)*
Miracle of God.

Natania, Netanya *(Nah-tahn-yah)*
Gift of God. Feminine form of Nathan.

Nataniella, Netaniella *(Nah-tahn-yel-ah)*
Gift of God. Feminine form of Nathaniel.

Nava *(Nah-vah)*
Beautiful.

Neah *(Nee-ah)*
A place name. (Joshua 19:13)

Nehama *(Neh-hahm-ah)*
Comfort. Feminine form of Nehemiah.

Neriah *(Ner-ee-yah, Ner-eye-ah)*
Light of the Lord. A man's name in the Bible; the father of Jeremiah's scribe, Baruch. (Jeremiah 32:12)

Netana *(Net-ahn-ah)*
Gift.

Netanela *(Net-ahn-el-la)*
Gift of God.

Nina, Neena
Granddaughter.

Nira *(Nee-rah)*
Light.

Nitza *(Neet-zah)*
Bud.

Noa
Tremble, shake. A daughter of Zelophehad. (Numbers 26:33)

Noadya *(Noh-ahd-yah, Noh-ah-dee-yah)*
Appointed by God. A prophetess. (Nehemiah 6:14)

Nofiya, Nophia *(Noh-fee-ya)*
God's beautiful landscape.

Ofira, Ophira
Gold. Feminine version of Ofir.

Ophrah, Ofra
Young deer or gazelle. A man's name; a descendant of Judah. (First Chronicles 4:14)

Ora
Light.

Orli, Oralee
My light.

Orna, Orni
Pine tree. Sometimes spelled Arna.

Orpah
To flee. Ruth's Moabite sister-in-law. (Ruth 1:4)

Pazya
God's gold.

Peninah *(Peh-nee-nah)*
Pearl or coral. Elkanah's second wife. (First Samuel 1:2)

Peri
Fruit.

Persis
A Greek name. A Christian woman of Roman descent. (Romans 16:12)

Philippa
Feminine version of Philip. Pippa is a nickname.

Phoebe
Shining. (Greek) A deaconess in the church at Cenchrea. (Romans 16:1)

Priscilla
Ancient. (Latin) Wife of Aquila, an early Christian in Corinth. (Acts 18:2)

Puah
To cry out. A midwife during the Egyptian captivity who disobeyed Pharaoh's order to kill all male Hebrews at birth. (Exodus 1:15)

Rachel
A ewe, symbol of gentleness and purity. Rachel was the beloved wife of Jacob, who gave birth to Joseph and Benjamin. (Genesis 29:16)

Rahama *(Reh-hahm-ah, Re-haym-ah)*
Compassion. Feminine version of Raham, a descendant of Judah. (First Chronicles 2:44)

Rana, Rona
Joy or song.

Raomi *(Ray-oh-mee)*
Antelope. (Aramaic) The consort of Nahor, Abraham's brother. (Genesis 22:24)

Raphaela
God has healed. Feminine of Raphael.

Reba, Reva
Quarter. In the Bible, a man's name; a Midianite king. (Joshua 13:21)

Rebecca, Rebekah
Beautiful, or to tie or bind. The strong-willed wife of Isaac, and mother of Jacob and Esau. (Genesis 24:15) The Hebrew is Rivkah.

Rhoda
Rose. A servant of Mary and the mother of Mark. (Acts 12:13)

Rimona
Pomegranate. Feminine of Rimon, a biblical place name. (Joshua 15:32)

Rina *(Ree-nah)*
Joy or song.

Rona, Roni, Ronia
Joy or song.

Ruth
Friend. The daughter-in-law of Naomi, who becomes a Hebrew and is an ancestor of King David and thus of Jesus. (Ruth)

Saphira *(Sa-fee-rah)*
Sapphire. (Greek) Wife of Hananiah. Early Christian of Jerusalem. (Acts 5:1)

Sara, Sarah
Princess. Sarah was the wife of Abraham, and, at the age of 90, the mother of Isaac. (Genesis 17:15) Nicknames include Sari, Sarina.

Sarai
The original form of Sarah's name. (Genesis 11:29)

Sela
Rock or musical note.

Sera
Abundance. Daughter of Asher. (Genesis 46:17) Serach in Hebrew.

Serafina
To burn. From the same root as "seraphim," the angels surrounding God's throne.

Sharon
Flat country. An area of ancient Palestine where roses and oak trees grew. King Solomon wrote about the roses of Sharon. Sharona is a variation.

Shera, Shira *(Shee-rah)*
Song. Daughter of Ephraim. (First Chronicles 7:24)

Shifra
Beautiful. A midwife who disobeyed Pharaoh's order to kill all male Hebrews at birth. (Exodus 1:15)

Shiloh
The gift is God's. A biblical place name. (Joshua 21:2)

Shoshana
Rose or lily.

Shua
Noble. An Asherite woman. (First Chronicles 7:32)

Shulamit *(Shoo-lah-meet)*
Peace.

Sima
Treasure. (Aramaic) Also a variation on Simona.

Simona, Simone
To hear. The feminine of Simon.

Stephanie
Crown. Feminine version of Stephen.

Susannah
Lily. A beautiful woman wrongly accused of adultery in the apocryphal History of Susannah. Also a follower of Jesus. (Luke 8:3) Shoshanah is the Hebrew. Susan is a well-known variation.

Tabitha
Gazelle. (Aramaic. Dorcas in Greek.) A Christian woman of Jaffa. Peter restores her to life. (Acts 9:36)

Talia, Talya
Dew.

Talma
Hill. Akin to Talmai, the king of Geshur and father-in-law of King David. (Second Samuel 3:3)

Tamar, Tamara

Date palm; graceful. Judah's daughter-in-law, then wife. (Genesis 38:6) Also, a daughter of Absalom. (Second Samuel 13:1) Timora and Timura are variations.

Tavora

Tavor is a mountain south of the Galilee. This is the feminine version. (Judges 4:6)

Temah *(Teh-mah)*

A man's name in the Bible; one of the returnees from the Babylonian exile. (Ezra 2:53)

Temana, Temania

One who comes from the south. The feminine version of Temani, a member of the tribe of Judah. (First Chronicles 4:6)

Temima *(Teh-mee-mah)*

Honest.

Thaddea

Gift of God. (Greek) Feminine version of Thaddeus.

Theophila

Beloved of God. (Greek) Feminine version of Theophilus.

Tiferet *(Tee-fehr-et)*

Beautiful.

Timnah

Withhold. A place name, man's name, and also a woman's name; sister of Lothan. (Genesis 36:22)

Tiria, Tirya *(Teer-ee-yah, Teer-yah)*

To be awake. (Aramaic) A man's name; a member of the tribe of Judah. (First Chronicles 4:16)

Tirza *(Teer-zah)*

Cypress, also desirable. A daughter of Zelophehad. (Numbers 26:33)

Tola

Vermillion. A man's name in the Bible, a son of Issachar. (Genesis 46:13)

Tori

My turtledove.

Tova, Tovia

Good one. Feminine version of Tobias or Tobit. Usually Toby in English.

Uma (Oo-ma)

Nation.

Uriella *(Oo-ree-el-la)*
God is my light. Feminine of Uriel.

Uzza *(Oo-zah)*
Strength. Uz was a grandson of Shem. (Genesis 10:23)

Uzziela *(Oo-zee-el-la)*
God is my strength. Feminine of Uzziel.

Vaniah *(Vah-nee-ah)*
A man's name in the Bible, an Israelite in the time of Ezra. (Ezra 10:36)

Varda *(Vahr-dah)*
Rose. Variations include Vardia, Vardina.

Vashti *(Vahsh-tee)*
The beautiful, the desired. (Persian) Wife of the Persian king Ahauseurus who ultimately marries Esther. (Esther 1:9)

Vida *(Vee-dah)*
A diminutive of Davida.

Yael *(Yah-elle)*

To ascend. A Kenite woman in the time of Deborah. (Judges 4:17)

Yafia *(Yah-fee-yah)*

To shine forth. A son of King David. (Second Samuel 5:15)

Yaira *(Yah-ee-rah)*

To light up. Feminine form of Yair.

Yara *(Yah-rah)*

Forest. A descendant of King Saul, a man's name. (First Chronicles 9:42)

Yedida *(Yeh-deed-ah)*

Friend, beloved. The mother of Josiah, a king of Judah. (Second Kings 22:1) Yedidya is a variation that means "friend of God."

---

*Although there are many names that begin with the "y" sound in Hebrew, many of these are familiar as "j" names in English (i.e., Judith = Yehudit) and most are found under "j" in this book (Joanna, Jordana, etc.). The names here either follow English usage (i.e., Yocheved) or are simply more melodious with the original "y" sound.

Since Jah (Yah) means "God," many of these names are theophoric—referring to God.

Yehiela *(Yeh-hee-el-la)*
May God live. Feminine version of Yehiel.

Yimla
Good fortune. (Aramaic) The father of the prophet Michayahu. (First Kings 22:8)

Yimna
Good fortune. (Aramaic) A son of Asher and grandson of Jacob. (Genesis 46:17)

Yiriya *(Yee-ree-yah)*
God sees. A man's name in the Bible, an officer under King Zedekiah. (Jeremiah 37:13)

Yisha *(Yee-shah)*
Salvation.

Yocheved *(Yoh-keh-ved)*
God's glory. Yocheved was the mother of Moses, Aaron, and Miriam. (Exodus 6:20)

Zahara, Zehari
Brightness.

Zahava, Zahavi
Golden.

Zanoah
A place name. A town in Judah. (Joshua 15:34)

Zaza
Movement. (Money in Aramaic.) A son of Jonathan. (First Chronicles 2:33)

Zelah, Zella
Rib. A place name. (Second Samuel 21:14)

Zemira *(Zeh-mee-rah)*
Song or melody. Used as a man's name in the Bible; a member of the tribe of Benjamin. (First Chronicles 7:8)

Zerua
Wounded. Mother of King Jeroboam. (First Kings 11:26)

Zevida, Zevuda *(Zeh-vee-dah, Ze-voo-dah)*
Gift. The mother of King Jehoiakim of Judah. (Second Kings 23:36)

Zia *(Zee-ah)*
To tremble or to move. A son of the tribe of Gad. (First Chronicles 5:13)

Zilla
Shadow. Wife of Lamech, mother of Tubal-Cain. (Genesis 4:19)

Zilpah
To drop or trickle. One of Jacob's wives, mother of Gad and Asher. (Genesis 29:24) Zilpha is a variation.

Zipporah
Little bird. Moses' wife. (Exodus 2:21)

Ziva
Splendid, radiant.

Zivya
Deer, gazelle. Mother of King Yehoash. (Second Kings 12:1)

Ziza *(Zee-zah)*
Industrious. A descendant of Reuben; a man's name in the Bible. (First Chronicles 4:37)

Zora, Zorah
A variation on Sarah. (Dawn in Arabic.) Also a biblical place name. (Judges 13:2) Also, Zara.

Resources

There are dozens of baby name books available. These two are more comprehensive and scholarly than most.

The Complete Dictionary of English and Hebrew Names by Alfred J. Kolatch (Middle Village, N.Y.: Jonathan David Publishers, 1984). A volume of nearly 500 pages, Kolatch's book includes a remarkable index so that if you wish your baby's name to reflect a quality, such as compassion, you will find suggestions under that heading.

Dictionary of Proper Names and Places in the Bible by O. Odlain and R. Seguineau (Garden City, N.Y.: Doubleday & Company, 1981). A comprehensive list that includes virtually every biblical reference to each and every personal and place name in both the Hebrew and Christian Bible.

Notes

1. Eliade, Mircea, ed. *The Encyclopedia of Religion.* New York: Macmillan, 1987, vol.10, p. 300.

2. Eliade, p. 310. Council of Trent 1545-1563; the Catholic Church's counter-reformation response to the Protestant Reformation.

3. Kolatch, Alfred. *The Name Dictionary.* Middle Village, N.Y.: Jonathan David Publishers, 1967, p. xi.

4. Odelain, O., and Seguineau, R. *Dictionary of Proper Names and Places in the Bible.* Garden City, N.Y.: Doubleday, 1981, p. x.

5. See "Resources."

6. One of the sons of Benjamin. Numbers 26:39.

For People of All Faiths, All Backgrounds
ABOUT JEWISH LIGHTS PUBLISHING

People of all faiths and backgrounds yearn for books that attract, engage, educate and spiritually inspire.

Our principal goal is to stimulate thought and help all people learn about who the Jewish People are, where they come from, and what the future can be made to hold. While people of our diverse Jewish heritage are the primary audience, our books speak to people in the Christian world as well and will broaden their understanding of Judaism and the roots of their own faith.

We bring to you authors who are at the forefront of spiritual thought and experience. While each has something different to say, they all say it in a voice that you can hear.

Our books are designed to welcome you and then to engage, stimulate and inspire. We judge our success not only by whether or not our books are beautiful and commercially successful, but by whether or not they make a difference in your life.

We at Jewish Lights take great care to produce beautiful books that present meaningful spiritual content in a form that reflects the art of making high quality books. Therefore, we want to acknowledge those who contributed to the production of this book.

PRODUCTION
Maria O'Donnell

EDITORIAL & PROOFREADING
Sandra Korinchak

COVER DESIGN
Annette Compton, Woodstock, Vermont

BOOK DESIGN
Karen Savary, Deering, New Hampshire

TYPE
Set in Goudy and Janson
Karen Savary, Deering, New Hampshire

COVER PRINTING
Coral Graphics, Hicksville, New York

PRINTING AND BINDING
Book Press, Brattleboro, Vermont

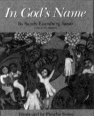

QUANTITY   **TOTAL**

_____ 11th Commandment (hc), $16.95	$_____
_____ But God Remembered (hc), $16.95	$_____
_____ God's Paintbrush (hc), $16.95	$_____
_____ In God's Name (hc), $16.95	$_____

For s/h add $3.50 for the first book, $2.00 for each
    additional book (to a max of $12.00),   s/h $_____

                                   TOTAL $_____

Check enclosed for $_____ payable to: JEWISH LIGHTS Publishing
Charge my credit card: ❑MasterCard   ❑Visa
Credit Card #_____Exp._____
Name on Card _____
Signature _____
Name _____
Street_____
City/State/Zip _____
Phone (_____)_____